9/09

Documenting World War II

Occupation and Resistance

Simon Adams

New York

Published in 2009 by The Rosen Publishing Group Inc.
29 East 21st Street, New York, NY 10010

First Edition

Editor: Camilla Lloyd
Consultant: Dr. R. Gerald Hughes and Dr. James Vaughan
Designer: Phipps Design
Picture researcher: Diana Morris
Maps: Ian Thompson
Indexer and proofreader: Patience Coster

Picture Acknowledgments: The author and publisher would like to thank the
following for allowing their pictures to be reproduced in this publication:
Cover: BL: Roger-Viollet/Getty Images, BR: Imperial War Museum, London;
Bettman/Corbis: 7; Cody Images: 10, 17, 18, 21, 22, 26, 31; Geoff Dann/DK
Images/Courtesy of IWM: 20; Mary Evans Picture Library: 1, 8, 11, 14, 28, 29, 30,
32, 33, 40, 42; Hulton Archive (Getty Images): 24, 25; Imperial War Museum,
London: 13, 15, 43; Keystone (Getty Images): 36, 44; Picturepoint/Topham: 6, 9, 39;
Roger-Viollet/Getty Images: 1, 16; Time & Life Pictures (Getty Images): 23.

Library of Congress Cataloging-in-Publication Data

Adams, Simon, 1955-
  Occupation and resistance / Simon Adams. -- 1st ed.
      p. cm. -- (Documenting World War II)
  Includes bibliographical references and index.
  ISBN 978-1-4042-1858-1 (lib. bdg.)
  1. World War, 1939-1945--Occupied territories. 2. World War, 1939-1945-
  -Underground movements. I. Title.
  D802.A2A33 2008
  940.53'36--dc22

                              2007041464

Manufactured in China

CONTENTS

World War II

During World War II (1939–45), Germany, Italy, and Japan occupied large parts of Europe, North Africa, and eastern Asia. For people living in the occupied countries, life under foreign rule was tough and brutal. Millions lost their lives, millions more lost their homes and jobs, and many became refugees as they fled to safety.

World War II (WWII) was in many ways a continuation of World War I (WWI, 1914–18). Germany had been defeated in that war, and emerged bitter and resentful at the harsh peace terms imposed on her at Versailles, France, in 1919. Both Italy and Japan had been on the winning side of the war, but they, too, were resentful that they had not gained enough status or territory in reward. All three countries felt cheated, and increasingly worked together to overthrow the peace settlement. They became known as the Axis powers, the name given to the German-Italian alliance of 1936 that later included Japan.

All three states were democracies, but in 1922, Italy became a fascist state under Benito Mussolini. The Nazi Party, an extreme fascist organization, took power in Germany in 1933 under the dictator Adolf Hitler. Japan became increasingly dominated by its armed forces.

During the 1930s, all three countries expanded their territory. Italy conquered Ethiopia in 1936 and Albania in 1939. Japan occupied the northern Chinese province of Manchuria in 1931 and then invaded the rest of China in 1937. Germany acquired Austria and the Sudeten border region of Czechoslovakia in 1938 and the rest of the country in 1939.

SOURCE

SPEECH

"Whether the other races live in comfort or perish of hunger interests me only in so far as we need them as slaves for our culture."

The German government's attitude to those people whose countries it occupied was brutal and self-serving.

Heinrich Himmler, head of the German SS, speaking in Poznan, Poland, October 1943.

WWII broke out in September 1939 when Germany invaded Poland. Britain and France declared war against Germany in support of Poland. Germany's long-term aim was to crush the Soviet Union, its main enemy and

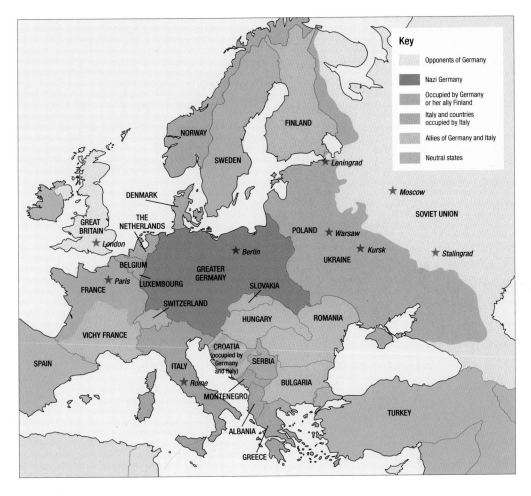

Key

Opponents of Germany

Nazi Germany

Occupied by Germany or her ally Finland

Italy and countries occupied by Italy

Allies of Germany and Italy

Neutral states

the world's foremost communist state, but it needed to make sure it did not have to fight in both Eastern and western Europe at the same time. In 1940, therefore, Germany turned west and invaded and occupied Norway, Denmark, Belgium, the Netherlands, Luxembourg, and France. It also occupied Yugoslavia and Greece in 1941 before turning east and invading the Soviet Union itself in June of that year.

In eastern Asia, Japan launched a surprise attack on the U.S. Navy at

German and Italian dominance in Europe and North Africa reached its greatest extent in the fall of 1942, when German troops were at the outskirts of Stalingrad and before the German defeat at El Alamein in North Africa and the invasion of northwest Africa by U.S. and British troops in November 1942.

Pearl Harbor in Hawaii in December 1941. Within a few months, Japan had overrun the whole of mainland Southeast Asia, Indonesia, and many Pacific islands, and even threatened Australia.

By the fall of 1942, the three allies—Germany, Italy, and Japan—were at the height of their powers.

Governing occupied Europe

Within the space of a few years, Germany and Italy had occupied most of Europe. Some countries welcomed or at least accepted their new rulers, but others were fiercely hostile. To control their new conquests, Germany and Italy set up new governments.

Germany swallowed the whole of Austria, western Poland, the Czech provinces of Bohemia and Moravia, and the eastern French provinces of Alsace and Lorraine. It called its vast new empire *Grossdeutsches Reich* (Greater Germany). German civilian governments ran Soviet Belarus, and the Baltic states of Estonia, Latvia, and Lithuania. German military governments ran the rest of the occupied Soviet Union and eastern Poland.

In western Europe, a variety of German-dominated governments was installed. Vidkun Quisling, a German collaborator, governed Norway as a "puppet state" of Germany. King Christian X and the government of Denmark remained in place, although they refused to collaborate with the Germans. *Reich* Commissioner Arthur Seyss-Inquart, the former Nazi leader of Austria, ran the civilian government of the Netherlands, and a German military government ran Belgium.

The German occupation of France (see pages 10–11) led to the division of the country. North and west France and the British-owned Channel Islands (see pages 12–13) were under military rule. Southern France—run from the small town of Vichy—became an independent state in collaboration with Germany.

In the Balkans, Italy expanded its territory along the eastern Adriatic coast and divided the rest of Yugoslavia and Greece with Germany. The pro-German, Ustase fascist government ran what is now Croatia and Bosnia.

Vidkun Quisling was the leader of the small Norwegian Fascist Party and formed a pro-German government after the German invasion of Norway in April 1940.

Bulgaria, Hungary, Romania, Slovakia, and the northern European state of Finland were independent, but allied to Germany and often took orders from it. All this might seem very complex, but in fact, the Germans were always in charge, even in some Italian-controlled areas. Not every country was occupied. Britain, and from 1941 its

Germany lost little time after its annexation of Austria in March 1938 to "Nazify" the country. Here, a notice has been posted in a Vienna shop window stating that the shop has been taken over by the Nazi Party's trade organization and that "Jews are not wanted."

allies, the Soviet Union, and the United States, fought on in opposition, while Portugal, Spain, Switzerland, Sweden, southern Ireland, and Turkey all remained neutral.

How Europe reacted

Most Europeans reacted to occupation with an understandable feeling of anger that their country had been invaded and conquered, and then resignation that there was nothing

Many people across Europe actively opposed German occupation. The Norwegian publication **Sannheten om Hakekorset,** *below, shows people who dared oppose the Germans being led away.*

they could now do about it. Faced with overwhelming German military might, most people bowed their heads and continued with their lives.

However, some people who shared the extreme views of the Nazis actively welcomed the occupiers. Fascist parties in Belgium, the Netherlands, and Croatia collaborated with Germany, and nationalists in Ukraine and the Baltic states welcomed the Germans as liberators from Soviet rule. More than 300,000 young Dutch, Belgian, French, Norwegian, and other nationalities were recruited into the German army. Many more supported the Germans in practical ways, such as giving information to the *Gestapo* (German secret police) about resistance fighters and other opponents, or supplying materials needed for the war effort.

The line between active collaboration with the enemy, on one hand, and passive acceptance of them on the other, was not always clear. A civil servant who had worked in, for example, the Dutch government might not want to continue working under German orders; but if he had a wife and family to support, he could not afford to resign from his job.

Likewise, a signalman working on the French railroads was only doing his job when he changed the signal from red to green. However, the train he allowed to pass might be full of German troops, or worse, Jews being taken to concentration camps (see pages 30–33). Were both these men actively collaborating with the Germans, or were they just doing their jobs and surviving the occupation?

A few people, as we shall see, actively opposed the occupation and joined resistance groups. Others fled into exile, many of them to Britain. So, too, did many of their governments. By 1941, the kings and queens of Norway, the Netherlands, Luxemburg, Greece, and Yugoslavia, the president of Czechoslovakia, the prime minister of Belgium, the former prime minister of Poland, and the leader of the Free French, Charles de Gaulle, were all living in London. These governments in exile were financially supported by Britain and used BBC radio station to broadcast messages to people at home.

SOURCE

SPEECH

"By vast superiority of the most modern arms, the enemy has been able to break our resistance. But ultimately, the Netherlands will rise again as a free nation. Long live our queen."

The Dutch Commander in Chief, General Henri Winkelman, ordering the Dutch people to surrender to the invading Germans in a broadcast on *Radio Hilversum*, May 14, 1940.

Strasbourg in eastern France had been part of Germany from 1871 to 1919, so it was unsurprising that many local people were happy that the German troops now occupied the city.

Occupied France

German armies first entered France on May 13, 1940 and had taken Paris by June 14. A week later, they occupied all but the far southern part of the country. In the face of this rapid advance, the French government collapsed. General Pétain, hero of the WWI resistance against the Germans at Verdun in 1916, took control. On June 22, he agreed an armistice with the Germans. France was divided in two, with the Germans occupying Paris, the north, and the entire important Atlantic coast, while the French continued to control the south of the country from their new capital at Vichy.

For France, this was a national humiliation. It was the third time since 1870 that France had been attacked by Germany, and as in 1871, it had again been forced to surrender. The Germans imposed military rule,

Hitler visited Paris on June 23, 1940, the day after the French had signed the humiliating armistice with Germany.

enforced a nightly curfew, introduced censorship, and restricted travel. They forbade demonstrations and strikes, and interned enemies of the state. Jews were particularly badly affected. In May 1941, 3,700 Jews were rounded up and held in camps around Paris; from March 1942, thousands of Jews were then transported across Europe to their deaths in extermination camps.

German soldiers quickly stripped French shops of luxury goods, such as perfume and cognac. Food was rationed, soap became a luxury item, and a shortage of leather meant that many people had to wear wooden clogs on their feet. Gasoline became unobtainable and coal and firewood difficult to find.

However, for many people the occupation made little difference. Shops, restaurants, and cafés soon reopened, nightclubs in Paris played to mixed German and French audiences, and many German soldiers soon found French girlfriends. In Vichy France, Marshal Pétain set up an authoritarian government and suppressed dissent. Nevertheless, life continued much as before until November 1942 when, following the Allied landings in Vichy-controlled North Africa, German troops occupied Vichy France and effectively ended its independence. Marshal Pétain became a "puppet" ruler with no real power.

RECOLLECTION

"Perhaps the most heart-rending sight of all was that of the German parades goose-stepping down the Champs Elysées every morning ... For every Frenchman, the Avenue reflected a glorious cavalcade of past victories —no one could bear to see it symbolizing defeat."

Polly Peabody, an American nurse working in Paris observed the Germans in Paris, in the fall of 1940.

PROPAGANDA POSTER

In unoccupied southern France, Marshal Pétain rallied his countrymen behind him in 1940: *"To each person his trade ... but for all: only one country: France; only one chief: Pétain."*

The Channel Islands

People in Britain like to think that they would have resisted a Nazi invasion in WWII, and refused to work with an imposed Nazi government. After all, Winston Churchill, wartime prime minister of Britain, had stated on June 4, 1940 that, faced with invasion, the British would fight and *"never surrender."* The experience of the Channel Islands—the only part of Britain to be occupied—suggests that things could have been different.

SOURCE

RECOLLECTION

"You couldn't stay enemies, living side by side for five years."

The reality of life on the islands was described by one resident.

Jersey housewife Kathleen Whitley, interviewed after the war.

After the surrender of France to the Germans in May 1940, it was inevitable that the Channel Islands, lying just off the northwest coast of France, would be invaded. On June 15, the British government began to demilitarize the islands. Thirty-thousand islanders, including the entire population of Alderney Isle, and all military equipment and personnel were shipped off to Britain, but 60,000 remaining islanders awaited their fate.

On June 30, German troops landed at Guernsey airport. The island surrendered, and the bailiff (head of government) issued a statement requesting that all German orders be obeyed and that no one resisted.

On July 1, the Germans occupied Jersey; the other smaller islands were occupied by July 3. Again, there was no resistance. The islands' governments continued as before, although all laws had to be submitted to the Germans for approval. The governments also carried out German orders, helping in the deportation of 2,200 U.K.-born islanders to camps in Germany, and enforcing anti-Jewish laws. The Guernsey government even handed over three Jewish women for deportation; all three later lost their lives in Auschwitz. At least three people were also deported from Jersey.

Generally, most islanders tolerated the occupying troops. They had little choice against such an overwhelming force, although they resented the curfews and rationing. Some openly collaborated but others objected, scrawling "V" signs on walls in July 1941 after British radio appealed for "V for

Victory" signs to be put up across occupied Europe.

Life became much harder for the islanders after D-Day in June 1944, when the islands were cut off from supplies from the French mainland. No bread was available and days without milk were common. The islanders faced starvation until the International Red Cross delivered food parcels at the end of the year.

By early 1945, the situation had become desperate as food ran out and

SOURCE

PHOTOGRAPH

After the "V for Victory" campaign on British radio BBC in summer 1941, Channel islanders opposed to German occupation began to paint "V" signs on German notices; if they were caught, penalties from the Germans were severe.

tension between occupiers and islanders rose. However, the Channel islanders could now look out across the narrow stretch of water separating them from France, and know that France had been liberated by the Allies. But the islanders had to wait. The Germans occupying the Channel Islands held out until the end of the war, their 27,000 soldiers only surrendered on May 9, two days after the rest of Europe.

Resistance!

Faced with occupation, many people learned to live under new masters, obeying their laws reluctantly and continuing their lives as best they could. Others, however, decided to resist in any way they could, for they were patriots who loved their country and wanted to set it free once again.

Resistance fighters were very clever at deceiving the enemy. This young French fighter might look like a farm worker, but he is actually smuggling arms and information via a horse and cart!

As soon as the German and Italian armies occupied a country, resistance groups sprang up. At first, these were small, locally organized groups but they soon developed a nationwide structure. Some, particularly in Eastern Europe and the Balkans, grew out of prewar communist parties, and others, such as *Milorg* in Norway and the Polish Home Army, were nationalist groups based around their governments in exile in London.

The most successful groups were those that had a wild, inaccessible landscape from which to operate: the mountains of Norway or Yugoslavia, the forested hills of Czechoslovakia, and the more remote parts of southern France. Resistance members came from all walks of life, and each one had a skill that could be used. At first, they produced documents telling people how to perform small acts of sabotage, such as printing illegal leaflets. They built up arms stores and gathered intelligence about the enemy. Later, they carried out large-scale acts of sabotage, such as blowing up trains.

Across Europe, the various groups received help from the British Special Operations Executive (the SOE; see pages 20–21) and the American Office of Strategic Services (OSS). The Russian State Security Service (NKVD) and Military Intelligence (GRU) sent support to communist groups fighting in Eastern Europe.

The success enjoyed by the various resistance groups was substantial. Greek fighters helped by British parachutists blew up the strategic Gorgopotamos bridge that carried the main rail line south to Athens. This severely disrupted the supply of weapons needed by the German General, Erwin Rommel, after his defeat at El Alamein in North Africa in November 1942. The Norwegian resistance spectacularly blew up the ferry carrying containers of "heavy water" (deuterium oxide), hindering any potential German atomic weapons research.

Resistance fighters were brave men and women, performing acts of sabotage and murder at great risk to their own lives. German informers were everywhere, and if the fighters were caught, the penalty for resistance was often death. On June 7, 1944, resistance fighters seized and liberated the town of Tulle in southwest France, and executed some Germans for allegedly being members of the *Gestapo*. Three days later, the Germans retook the town, hanging 99 citizens from lampposts and trees in the square.

French resistance fighters performed acts of sabotage, such as blowing up railroad lines. They often had great success, although they faced certain death if they were caught by the Germans.

RECOLLECTION

"We gave hints, like 'If you want to put a German car out of action, pour sugar into the fuel tank. Or [throw] three-headed nails in front of the German cars.'"

Resistance groups gave out advice to prospective saboteurs in hastily printed pamphlets.

Philippe de Vomécourt, one of the first members of the French Resistance.

The French Resistance

One of the most successful resistance movements emerged in France during the German occupation in May to June 1940. Local groups hurriedly helped Allied airmen escape back to Britain and helped Jews fleeing the Nazis to find safety in neutral Spain or Switzerland.

Different groups soon sprang up. However, they remained disunited since many French people accepted the Vichy government's authority in unoccupied southern France. Also, General de Gaulle's attempts to lead a "Free French" movement based in London were not well received at first. The various groups came together in May 1943 under the National Council of Resistance (CNR), although the French communist party maintained its own military forces.

The French resistance had the advantage of being geographically close to Britain. The Royal Air Force could drop in supplies and agents, and information and foreign agents could be smuggled out in French fishing boats or British submarines. By 1944, the resistance had grown in strength to about 400,000 members. The groups had many successes. Fighters in Brittany in northwest France paralyzed German communications before the D-Day landings in June 1944, and groups in Normandy and the south of France attacked German troops after the Allied invasion of France.

In 1942 René Duchez, a house painter and courier for the Century network in Normandy, made a

SOURCE

PROPAGANDA

After 23 communist resistance fighters—many of them foreigners to France—were caught and executed in Paris by the Germans in February 1944, the authorities produced this red poster identifying the men as communists, Jews, and foreigners responsible for many crimes. In this way, they hoped to undermine the claims of the Resistance to be fighting for France.

remarkable discovery. As he repainted a German major's office in Caen, he noticed a large map on the desk. He hid it behind a mirror, and later smuggled it out and gave it to the head of the network in a local bar. The map was a detailed plan of the Le Havre to Cherbourg section of the "Atlantic wall," the German fortification built to protect France from an Allied invasion. The map was taken to England hidden in a cookie can on board a trawler and was invaluable in the preparations for D-Day, the Allied invasion of France.

Women played a key role in the resistance, since they were less conspicuous than men. They drove cars, acted as couriers, kept safe houses to shelter agents, and organized many local groups. Marie-Madeleine Fourcade worked as a secretary at a major Paris publishing house and directed the 3,000-strong Alliance network of agents. Odette Sansom sailed across the Mediterranean from Gibraltar in a *felucca*—an Egyptian sailing boat—and worked as courier with a resistance group in southern France. Violette Szabo was recruited by Britain's SOE (see pages 20–21) and twice parachuted into France to set up networks of agents. On her second mission, she worked with the local resistance leader to help coordinate sabotage missions around D-Day. Unfortunately, she was captured by the Germans and died in Ravensbruck concentration camp in January 1945.

Her fate was not uncommon, for an estimated 150,000 French people lost their lives fighting to free their country from the Nazis.

RECOLLECTION

"I ask you to believe me when I say that the cause of France is not lost … Whatever happens, the flame of French resistance must not and shall not die."

General de Gaulle in a broadcast to the French people from London just after the fall of France, BBC radio, June 18, 1940.

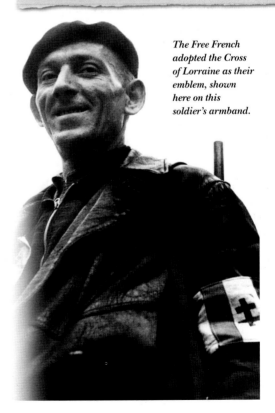

The Free French adopted the Cross of Lorraine as their emblem, shown here on this soldier's armband.

Spies and spying

While a traditional war was being fought by armed forces on land, sea, and in the air, another equally important war was being fought in secret. This was the war between the combatants' intelligence services, since each side used spies to find out what the other side was up to.

At the start of the war, Britain, Germany, the Soviet Union, and Japan had extensive intelligence networks of spies working abroad. The United States had kept out of world affairs since the end of WWI in 1918, and so had few such networks, although it quickly made up for lost time. All the networks had to adapt quickly to the new wartime conditions.

The main role of spies in wartime is to provide intelligence about an enemy's plans and movements. Their other role is to dupe the enemy into believing wrong information about the opposing country's plans. Such work requires great nerve, and many agents were captured and killed during WWII. Others were "turned," that is captured

The first Enigma machine had only three rotors, but later versions had four. This German machine was captured in France by the U.S. Army in 1944.

by the enemy and made to work for their captor by sending back misleading information to their former masters. It is not surprising that the information sent by spies was often false or not believed.

One of the most successful spies of WWII was Richard Sorge, a German journalist who spied for the Soviet Union. In 1933, he went to Japan as a foreign correspondent for the *Frankfurter Zeitung* newspaper. He gained the confidence of the German ambassador in Tokyo and regularly sent information to Moscow about German and Japanese plans. In May 1941, he warned the Soviet Union of its forthcoming invasion by Germany. The Soviet leader, Josef Stalin, did not believe him. Stalin also did not believe Sorge when he said that Japan was more interested in invading Southeast Asia than in attacking the Soviet Union. When intelligence picked up by intercepting German secret messages confirmed this report, Stalin moved his army divisions away from defending the east of the country to halt the German invasion in the west.

The Germans, too, had some successful spies, notably Cicero, a valet to the British ambassador to neutral Turkey. Cicero gained information about the Allied leaders' planning meetings in Tehran in November 1943, held to discuss the invasion of France, and sent it back to Germany. The Germans did not believe him and paid

SOURCE

THE ENIGMA MACHINE

The Enigma machine was a mechanized electrical device used by the Germans for enciphering and deciphering military and diplomatic messages. The machine enciphered each letter of each word separately through a series of plug connections and rotors. When it was enciphered, the complete message was then sent via radio to a receiver, where it was deciphered using another machine. The complexity of the Enigma process made it very difficult for the British to break its code, especially since the Germans kept altering the machine to make it more complex. However, a team of codebreakers—including the brilliant mathematician, Alan Turing—working at Bletchley Park in Britain produced a series of the electromechanical devices known as "Bombes," which successfully broke the code. The British were thus able to read German naval intelligence about U-boat movements in the North Atlantic and could direct Allied shipping away from danger.

him with forged money. Cicero was jailed for passing forged notes, and later died in poverty. Had the Germans believed this information, the course of the war might have been different.

The SOE

One of the most successful secret organizations operating in wartime Europe was the Special Operations Executive (SOE). Set up by the British prime minister, Winston Churchill, in July 1940, the SOE's task was to equip, train, and help resistance groups in Europe and to carry out sabotage operations.

SOE agents received rigorous training in Britain, learning such skills as burglary, safe-breaking, industrial sabotage, hand-to-hand combat, and silent killing. The agents were supplied with forged papers produced by the Science Museum and clothes suitable for the country in which they would be operating. They were also equipped with an "L" ("lethal") cyanide pill to take if they were captured; this would kill them in seconds and thus avoid the risk of them giving valuable secrets away under torture. The agents were then parachuted or flown into occupied territory to start work.

The first SOE missions often went spectacularly wrong. When the wireless operator, Hubert Lauwers,

was sent to the Netherlands to help the resistance groups there, he was captured by the Germans and forced to transmit false signals back home. He deliberately left out his agreed security check, but the British stupidly ignored this omission every time. Between 1942–1943, they therefore sent 52 more SOE agents along with vast quantities of arms and explosives to be captured by the Germans. Eventually, two of the agents escaped back home and alerted the British of their mistake. Nevertheless, the SOE had success in other areas. In May 1942, two resistance fighters assassinated

SOE agents were not allowed to carry anything that might betray their true identity. This matchbox might look French, but it was actually produced in Britain for SOE agents to use when they worked in France.

Reinhard Heydrich, the tyrannical Nazi ruler of western Czechoslovakia in an operation masterminded by the SOE. However, the German response was swift, and resulted in the murder of the entire population of two nearby villages as well as many resistance fighters, a total of over 5,000 people.

Some of the SOE exploits were incredibly daring. In April 1944, two SOE agents, Patrick Leigh Fermor and Stanley Moss, were sent to Crete. Dressed in German uniforms, they waved red lights to halt the car of General Kreipe, the German divisional

commander. They hit the driver on the head, kidnapped the general, and drove him past 24 guard posts before making off into the mountains. The general was eventually smuggled off the island by submarine to Cairo. By this stage of the war, sabotage and acts of resistance were common, as Europe truly was, in Churchill's words, *"set ablaze."*

This is a montage of forged stamps used by the SOE to make false identities and permits.

Partisans

In some parts of Europe, resistance fighters formed guerrilla armies to fight the German occupiers. These partisans, as they were known, fought with arms supplied by the Allies or captured from the Germans. They enjoyed considerable success.

Tito's partisans fighting the Germans in Yugoslavia were among the most effective resistance groups in all of Europe. Here a group advances cautiously along a road, wary of German attack.

The main areas of partisan activity were in Yugoslavia, Albania, Greece, Poland, behind the German lines in the Soviet Union, and after 1943, in Italy. The partisans were all highly motivated; many of them were extreme nationalists trying to restore their prewar governments, or communists seeking to introduce a communist government after the war. They operated in small, highly mobile units

and lived in inaccessible terrain, such as mountains and forests. Attacks often took the Germans by surprise, for the partisans knew their territory well and quickly retreated to their hideouts to plan their next operation.

The most successful partisan armies operated in Yugoslavia. After the German invasion of April 1941, two main armies led the resistance—the pro-royal, anti-communist *Chetnik* resistance fighters and the communist-led partisans of Josip Broz Tito. The two factions soon argued and began to fight each other. When the *Chetniks* turned to their former enemies, Germany and Italy, for support, the British threw their full weight behind Tito's partisans and supplied them with arms and agents.

By early 1944, Tito was in command of 300,000 partisans and controlled much of the country. As the Soviet Red Army moved across Eastern Europe, the partisans attacked, taking the Yugoslav capital, Belgrade, with Soviet support, and liberated almost all their country by the war's end. Communist partisans led by Enver Hoxha enjoyed similar success in Albania, and liberated their entire country.

The vast expanses of the Soviet Union allowed huge partisan groups to operate successfully in German-occupied territory. The groups had at least 250,000 members, who disrupted

SOURCE

POSTER

This Soviet propaganda poster, produced in 1941, praised the Soviet partisans fighting behind German lines, stating that, "*partisans beat the enemy without mercy.*" The Soviet partisan oath was:
"*For the towns and villages burnt down, for the death of our women and children, for the torture, violence, and humiliation wreaked on my people, I swear to take revenge …*"

German supply lines, wrecked 18,000 trains, and killed or wounded thousands of German soldiers. Similar successes were enjoyed by the 200,000 anti-fascist partisans in Italy, who fought the German troops occupying the country after the Italians surrendered to the Allies in September 1943. Italian partisans even captured and killed the former leader, Mussolini, in April 1945.

Life in Nazi Germany

The war did not just affect those people under occupation. It also affected the Germans. Most of them greeted the outbreak of war with apprehension, although their daily lives were little changed. By 1943, the German people too began to suffer great hardships.

The outbreak of war brought food and then clothes rationing, with the poor receiving extra food rations. *Hamstern* ("hamstering," or hoarding) became a national obsession, although soldiers sent back food and clothes from the occupied territories, and Dutch dairy produce and luxury items,

The civilians of Koblenz in Germany line up in front of bombed-out buildings for rations in 1945. Hildegarde Knef of Berlin remembered the effect of Allied bombing on the city: the distinctive "smell of burning, and sweet, fatty smell of the buried, not yet dug out."

such as French silks and Norwegian furs also flooded in. As had been the case before the war, most women did not work and stayed at home. Most people continued to go to the movies or theater and enjoyed holidays by the sea or in the mountains.

This situation changed for the worse in the winter of 1941–42. So many farm workers were now fighting in the Soviet Union that Germany began to run out of food. Bread and meat rations were cut and the daily diet became poorer. The Allied bombing of cities from 1942 also brought the reality of war home to many Germans. After Hamburg was destroyed in a bombing raid in July 1943, more than 800,000 people—two-thirds of the population—had to be evacuated. Meanwhile, the constant bombing of Berlin reduced every third house to rubble.

After the German defeat at Stalingrad in February 1943, Josef Goebbels, the Nazi propaganda minister, announced "total war" measures to win the war. All men between the ages of 16 and 65 were registered for compulsory labor, youths aged between 10 and 15 were sent to work on farms, and millions of women were conscripted into industry and civil defense, where they operated antiaircraft searchlights and even fired

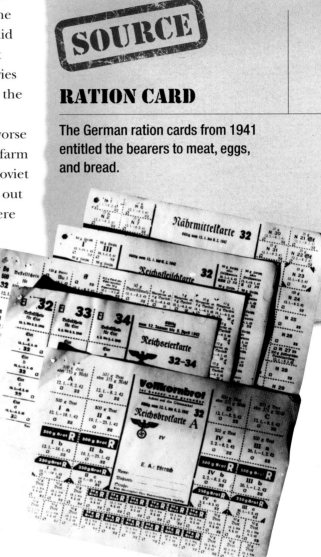

SOURCE

RATION CARD

The German ration cards from 1941 entitled the bearers to meat, eggs, and bread.

the guns. As a result of these and other efforts, the production of armaments had quadrupled by the middle of 1944. Such measures did not, however, save Germany from defeat. By the end of the war, food was very scarce and many people looted food stores and freight trains in order to survive.

Opposing Hitler

It would be a mistake to see every German as a card-carrying member of the Nazi Party. Most Germans remained outside the party but supported the Nazi leader, Adolf Hitler, because he was the leader of their nation and they were patriots. Others, however, were opponents of the Nazi regime and paid for their opposition with their lives.

The Nazis absorbed some sympathetic political parties but banned the communists, socialists, and others who opposed them within a few months of taking power in January 1933. Trade unions and most political organizations were outlawed. The *Gestapo* crushed all opposition to the regime, imprisoning opponents or sending them to their deaths in concentration camps.

Hitler (foreground, right) shows Mussolini (foreground, left) the damage to his headquarters in eastern Germany after an attempt on his life in July 1944.

Both the Protestant and Catholic churches in Germany largely supported the Nazi regime, since they were conservative organizations frightened by the rise of communism, and they supported Hitler's attempts to impose social order and authority on the country. However, many church groups and individual churchmen were brave enough to oppose the regime and speak out against it. In the summer of 1941, the Catholic bishop of Munster denounced the murder of mentally and physically disabled adults and children. His opposition ended the T4 "euthanasia program," as it was called. A few months later individual priests, notably Martin Niemöller and Dietrich Bonhoeffer, preached against Nazi atrocities and the persecution of the Jews.

Opposition to the Nazi regime grew as the war turned against Hitler. In February 1943, 4,000 students at Munich University shouted down the district governor of Bavaria when he criticized the students for not joining the army; demonstrations and riots followed. An underground resistance group, the *Weisse Rose* ("White Rose") circulated leaflets and pasted up anti-Nazi posters in the university. This campaign spread to about a dozen cities before the Nazis arrested and executed its leading members.

The main opposition to Hitler came from within the army, because many senior soldiers felt that Hitler was leading them to inevitable defeat. In July 1944, Colonel Claus von Stauffenberg placed a bomb beneath Hitler's conference table at his headquarters at Rastenburg in eastern

SOURCE

RECOLLECTION

"Do you known that in the future teeth are going to be pulled through the nose?"

"Why?"

"Because nobody dares open his mouth!"

Anti-Nazi jokes circulated in Germany. They were known as *Flusterwitze*, "whispered jokes," because it was dangerous to tell them openly in public.

Germany. The bomb exploded but did not kill Hitler. Countermeasures taken by Hitler's supporters in Berlin crushed the conspiracy, and allowed Hitler to retain power until his suicide in April 1945 and Germany's defeat.

More than 5,000 people were executed for their part in the bomb plot, including Dietrich Bonhoeffer and Admiral Wilhelm Canaris, the former head of *Abwehr*, the military intelligence department, of which many members were opposed to Hitler.

Life in Eastern Europe

Although life under occupation in western Europe was sometimes brutal, most people were treated better than those in the east as the Germans had some respect for them as humans. The same was not true in Eastern Europe. The Nazis believed the Germans to be an Aryan master race of fair-haired, light-skinned people who should rule the world. Those in the east—the Slavs, and above all, the Jews—were seen as subhumans, who could be cleared out of the way to make *lebensraum* ("living space") for the German master race.

The effects of this racist policy were horrific. As German armies marched eastward, first into Poland and then the Soviet Union, national governments were swept away. Poland disappeared from the map and was absorbed into Germany, and the rest of the region fell under German military or civil administration. Following the troops came the *Einsatzgruppen*, special "action groups" of the SS, who shot every communist and Jew they could find on the spot.

The scale of this killing was immense. Hundreds of thousands of Poles and Russians were shot and their homes and belongings seized, and many thousands more were evicted from their homes to make way for German settlers. The violence directed at them was indiscriminate and disorganized, according to German military demands in the area. Much more deliberate, however, was the

This peasant in Russia was flogged for refusing to hand over food to the Nazis. Those suspected of supporting the partisans were shot on the spot, or hanged to serve as a warning to others.

The Nazis behaved with great brutality throughout Eastern Europe. They burned villages and farms to the ground, such as this one in Ukraine, either to prevent enemy troops using them as shelter, or as a reprisal action against local partisans.

systematic killing of the Jews (see pages 30–31). In 1941 alone, more than 500,000 Jews were killed by German soldiers, policemen, and local Nazi sympathizers in the Baltic states, Belarus, and Ukraine. Millions more were to die during the Holocaust.

The peoples of Eastern Europe suffered twice, once as the German army invaded and then, from 1943 onward, as the German army retreated in the face of the liberating Red Army. Entire towns and villages were wiped off the map forever, and whole cities were razed to the ground. The death toll from all this carnage was immense. More than 20 million Russians lost their lives, and Poland lost 6.6 million people, one-fifth of its total prewar population.

RECOLLECTION

"The bodies were lying so closely packed together that only their heads showed ... The ditch was already three-quarters full. I estimate that it held about a thousand bodies."

The *Einsatzgruppen* used extreme, brutal methods to get rid of their enemies.

Herman Gräbe, a German builder, remembers the actions of the *Einsatzgruppen*.

The Jews of Europe

The Nazis came to power in 1933 with an anti-Semitic program. No one expected, however, just what horrors they would unleash on the Jews of Europe.

The Nazis moved quickly against the Jews of Germany, attacking their businesses, removing them from the civil service, judiciary, schools, and universities, and sending some to concentration camps such as Dachau. The Nuremberg Laws of 1935 stripped Jews of their citizenship and forbade them to marry Germans; sexual relationships between Jews and non-Jews were strictly forbidden.

Attacks against Jews came to a head in November 1938, when 7,500 Jewish shops were attacked and synagogues burned on *Kristallnacht* ("the Night of Broken Glass"). Many Jews tried to leave Germany, but few countries would take them. By the outbreak of war in 1939, however, half the 500,000 Jews living in Germany in 1933 had managed to flee abroad.

The invasion of Poland in 1939 brought two million more Jews under Nazi control. Most were rounded up and herded into ghettos in the major towns; these ghettos were walled up and fenced off to prevent the Jews

There was so little food in the Warsaw ghetto and other ghettos that their Jewish residents were forced to beg for food on the streets. Life in the Warsaw ghetto was hard even for children. Stanislaw Rozykzi, a Polish Jew who lived in the Warsaw ghetto wrote: **"On the streets children are crying in vain, children who are dying of hunger … without underwear, without clothing, without shoes. … already completely grown up at the age of five, gloomy and weary of life."**

IDENTITY CARD

Across Europe, Jews were issued with identity cards, which they had to carry with them at all times. The Vichy French authorities issued this card in February 1942.

from escaping. Other Jews were sent to work in labor camps along the Soviet border, where they dug trenches and built fortifications. Many were simply killed.

The same fate befell many Soviet Jews who fell under Nazi rule after Germany invaded the Soviet Union in 1941. Groups of SS *Einsatzgruppen* troops killed as many Jews as they could find; some were gassed in mobile gas vans built specially for the purpose. However, it soon became clear that the use of murder squads and ghettos would not be enough to clear the occupied areas of all Jews. The Nazis therefore devised the "Final Solution,"

building large-scale death camps to gas thousands of Jews at a time. Six such camps were built, the most notorious being Auschwitz. At least 1.6 million Jews were killed in these camps. A total of 6 million Jews, more than half the entire Jewish population of Europe—one-third of all Jews in the world—lost their lives under the Nazis.

Forced labor

Throughout the war, millions of people from all the occupied countries in Europe were forced to work for the Germans, producing materials needed for the war. Most of these workers were treated little better than slaves, and millions died of overwork, hunger, and disease.

Soon after they came to power in 1933, the Nazis set up concentration camps to house political prisoners, Jews, gypsies, and other "enemies of the state." Many of these inmates were set to work in nearby factories and mines, and were often worked to death. After the war started in 1939, the Nazis began to build specific labor, or work camps, where the sole purpose was to provide a workforce for the war effort. Some 127 work camps were set up in Poland alone, with many more established in other occupied countries as well as in Germany itself.

The concentration and new labor camps provided a workforce for hundreds of well-known German firms,

The conditions in which forced laborers—such as these inmates of Auschwitz—were forced to live were appalling, and many quickly died of hunger and disease. Rudolf Höss, commandant of Auschwitz remembered: **"Every month, one-fifth died or were, because of inability to work, sent back … to the camps … to be exterminated."**

Prisoners held in German labor camps were forced to work on reclaiming the land and turning it into farmland for the Germans.

including the aircraft builders Messerschmitt, Heinkel, and Junkers, motor makers Daimler-Benz and BMW, and electrical firms such as Siemens. Slave laborers produced arms, ammunition, tanks, airplanes, steel, cement, and many other items. They worked in quarries and mines to produce the necessary raw materials, and labored on the land to grow food. Many were also put to work repairing buildings damaged by Allied bombing. Since all able-bodied German men were fighting in the armed services, the demand for slave labor was vast.

The workers consisted of four main groups: prisoners of war; concentration camp inmates; Jews, Poles, Russians, and others from Eastern Europe; and large numbers of foreign civilians from occupied countries in western Europe who had been forced to move to Germany and work against their will for the enemy. The numbers involved were vast: some 7 million people were enslaved by 1944, 800,000 civilians from France alone. There were few who could survive the hard work, long hours, and lack of food, and those who could not, died or were quickly killed in nearby death camps. The number of slave workers to lose their lives is unknown, but the death toll was immense. Thirty-thousand Jews died while they worked at the IG Farben petrochemical works at Auschwitz, and at least three million Soviet prisoners of war were worked to death.

The Land of the Rising Sun

On the other side of the world from Europe, a different war was being waged by Japan. "The Land of the Rising Sun," as a name for Japan, comes from Japan's position to the east of China. From the Chinese point of view, the sun rises from Japan. This name has become a popular Western description of Japan. Allied to Germany and Italy since 1936–37, Japan carved out a massive empire throughout eastern and Southeast Asia and across the Pacific Ocean.

Although on the victorious side in WWI, Japan felt cheated by the Versailles Treaty of 1919, because it believed it was treated as a second-class power by both Britain and the U.S. Japan wanted an empire that would guarantee its security and provide its industry with the raw materials it did not have, such as oil and rubber. The military and the extreme nationalists, increasingly dominant in the government, promoted this policy. In November 1938, prime minister Konoe proposed a "New Order" in east Asia, in which Japan would work with China to resist communist and Western interference in the region. In effect, Japan proposed to run China for its own military and economic ends. The New Order was later expanded to include British, French, and Dutch colonies in Southeast Asia and the U.S.-owned Philippines. All these countries were to form a Great East Asia Co-Prosperity Sphere, an economically self-sufficient region of "*coexistence and co-prosperity.*" Again, this sphere was to be dominated by Japan.

By the outbreak of war in Europe in 1939, Japan had already occupied the northern Chinese province of Manchuria in 1931 and invaded the rest of China in 1937. Its aggressive policies and hostility toward communism made it a natural ally for Germany, with which it signed the Anti-Comintern Pact against the Soviet Union in 1936. Like Germany, it, too, signed a nonaggression pact with the Soviet Union in April 1941. This meant that Japan was able to operate freely throughout eastern Asia without fear of Soviet intervention.

In July 1941, Japan stationed troops in the French colony of Indo-China. The U.S., British, and the Dutch government in exile in London, which was still governing the Dutch East Indies (now Indonesia), retaliated by suspending all financial and trading relations with Japan, thereby cutting off 90 percent of Japan's fuel supplies.

In order to protect its own interests and expand its empire, Japan went on the offensive. In December 1941, it

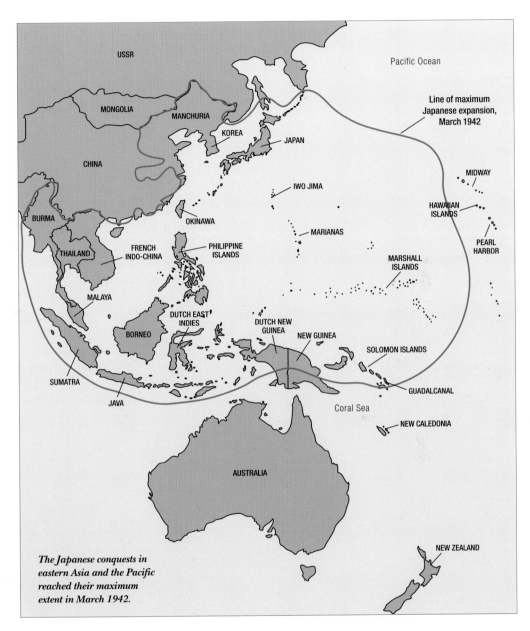

USSR

Pacific Ocean

MONGOLIA

MANCHURIA

Line of maximum
Japanese expansion,
March 1942

KOREA

JAPAN

CHINA

MIDWAY

IWO JIMA

HAWAIIAN
ISLANDS

BURMA

OKINAWA

MARIANAS

PEARL
HARBOR

THAILAND

FRENCH
INDO-CHINA

PHILIPPINE
ISLANDS

MARSHALL
ISLANDS

MALAYA

DUTCH EAST
INDIES

DUTCH NEW
GUINEA

NEW GUINEA

SUMATRA

BORNEO

SOLOMON ISLANDS

GUADALCANAL

JAVA

Coral Sea

NEW CALEDONIA

AUSTRALIA

NEW ZEALAND

*The Japanese conquests in
eastern Asia and the Pacific
reached their maximum
extent in March 1942.*

launched a surprise attack on the U.S. fleet at Pearl Harbor, thereby bringing the United States into the war. It followed up this attack with a series of successful invasions of Burma, Malaya, Singapore, the Dutch East Indies, Sarawak, Brunei, the Philippines, New Guinea, and numerous Pacific islands. These invasions saw Japan extend its empire from the borders of British India in the west, down almost to Australia in the south and across the Pacific Ocean in the east. The world war had now become truly global.

Life under Japanese rule

The Japanese conquest of Southeast Asia brought 150 million people under its rule. Many of them welcomed the Japanese as liberators, although they later came to regret their support.

In Europe, Germany, and Italy invaded and occupied independent nations. The Japanese, however, with

the exception of China, occupied European or American colonies, such as British Burma, French Indo-China, the Dutch East Indies, and the American Philippines. Many people, therefore, welcomed the Japanese as Asian liberators from European rule. In theory, the Japanese treated their new empire with respect. Local leaders ran the former colonies, and both Burma and the Philippines became

Five Chinese prisoners of war are buried alive by Japanese captors just outside Nanking after the fall of the Chinese capital in 1937.

nominally independent from Japan in 1943. All the countries in the empire were represented in the Greater Asia Council, which met in Tokyo in November 1943, and the entire empire was linked together within the Great East Asia Co-Prosperity Sphere (see pages 34–35).

The reality, however, was that Japan remained in full control. Every part of the empire flew the Japanese flag, used Japanese money, and kept to local Tokyo time. All public meetings began with a bow to the Japanese emperor, Hirohito.

Children learned Japanese, all Western languages were prohibited, although English or French continued to be used as the common language in most places, and all American music and movies were banned. Nonapproved political parties were outlawed, censorship was introduced, and everyone had to carry an identity card and needed a special pass to travel anywhere.

Japanese rule was often extremely brutal. More than 250,000 civilians were massacred when the Japanese captured the Chinese capital of Nanking in 1937, and many thousands more people were killed during the Japanese advances in 1941 and 1942. The Japanese also used biological weapons against the Chinese. In Manchuria, the Japanese performed hideous medical experiments on Chinese prisoners.

RECOLLECTION

"The Japanese behaved like animals whose language we could not understand."

S.C. Goho, president of the Indian Association of Singapore, 1940s.

The *Kempeitai* (military police) kept order by beating and torturing local people. The victims of the *Kempeitai* were hung by their wrists and tortured with electricity and chemicals. Prisoners of war were treated with extreme cruelty (see pages 38–39).

The Japanese also bled their empire dry, using up all its oil, rice, and other products. As a result, food became scarce. At least 400,000 Vietnamese lost their lives from famine in 1944–45, as did many more in the Philippines and Malaya. Thousands also lost their lives as slave laborers, since all men aged between 16 and 40 years were rounded up in the Dutch East Indies, Malaya, and Burma, and forced by the Japanese to build roads and railroads, or work in factories and farms.

Unsurprisingly, major revolts broke out throughout the areas that Japan controlled: in Burma, the Dutch East Indies, French Indo-China, and the Philippines.

Prisoners of the Empire

The rapid Japanese advance through Southeast Asia in 1941–42 took the Allies by surprise. Thousands of Allied troops were captured and spent the rest of the war as POWs (prisoners of war). For them, life was very brutal.

SOURCE

RECOLLECTION

"We have had face-slapping incidents and cases of brutality; I have seen prisoners beaten to the ground with rifle butts."

Life as a Japanese prisoner of war was hard and often brutal.

POW David Nelson in Changi camp, Singapore, March 31, 1942.

The Geneva Convention of 1929 guaranteed that POWs should receive food, clothing, medical treatment, and regular exercise. It also set out the maximum penalty of 30 days in solitary confinement if they tried to escape. Japan, however, had not signed the convention and so kept its POWs in appalling conditions without any regard for their health or welfare.

One of the most brutal regimes was the Changi camp in Singapore, where 50,000 British and Commonwealth soldiers were imprisoned after the Japanese took the British island fortress in February 1942. At first the Japanese let the prisoners look after themselves, since they had nowhere to escape to. Conditions deteriorated, however, when Koreans and troops from the Indian National Army replaced the front-line Japanese troops. The Indian nationalist army allied with the Japanese in order to win India's independence from Britain. Food soon became scarce at the camp, and by the war's end, the inmates were eating seaweed and whatever food they could scavenge. A total of 8,000 of the 22,000 Australian soldiers captured by the Japanese died; 12,500 of the 50,000 British soldiers met the same fate.

Many of these prisoners died while working as slave laborers. The Japanese used forced labor to build roads, bridges, and railroads. Most notorious was the construction of the 258-mile (415-km) railroad between Thailand and Burma that ran through thick jungle and along treacherous mountain ridges alongside the Kwai Nok river. More than 61,000 British, Dutch, American, and Australian prisoners labored on the railroad, alongside thousands of Chinese, Thai, and Burmese workers. The Japanese treated these workers with particular

brutality, making them toil from dawn
to dusk in the extreme heat and
monsoon conditions. By the time the
railroad was completed, in October
1943, 12,000 POWs and 90,000 Asian

*Conditions for prisoners working on the Thailand-Burma
railroad were atrocious. Many of them died from
malnutrition or tropical diseases between 1942–43.*

workers had died, one for each 13 feet
(4 meters) of track.

Awaiting liberation

Across Europe and Asia, occupied countries eagerly awaited their liberation by the Allies. The wait was often long, since both the Germans and Japanese were heavily armed, skilled fighters, defending their gains with great courage and determination.

In April 1943, the Germans began to close the Warsaw ghetto and deport its inhabitants to the death camps. Even children were rounded up to be sent to the camps and some to death.

After the three great Allied victories of 1942–43—the Battle of the Coral Sea (May 1942) and Midway (June 1942), where Japanese ambitions were checked by the U.S.; the British defeat of the Germans and Italians at El Alamein in November 1942; and the Soviet defeat of the Germans at Stalingrad in February 1943—it was clear that the tide of war had turned

against the Axis powers. However, it was also clear that neither the Germans nor the Japanese would surrender an inch of ground. As a result, no one knew when the war would end.

Across Europe, resistance work increased, partisan activity was stepped up, and strikes and demonstrations against German rule became more common. Danish resistance to German domination led to numerous strikes and acts of sabotage during 1943. When the Danish government refused to pass repressive measures against its people, the Germans imposed direct rule. The Danish navy then scuttled its entire fleet. The introduction of anti-Semitic legislation in October 1943—under which the Germans planned to deport all Danish Jews to their deaths in concentration camps—met with effective resistance. Danish sea captains and fishermen ferried all but 500 of Denmark's 8,400 Jews to safety in neutral Sweden.

In Eastern Europe, the Jews of the Warsaw ghetto fought back as the Germans started to close the ghetto in April 1943. The Germans retaliated by burning down the ghetto building by building. By mid-May, the entire ghetto had been razed: 56,000 Jews had been killed or deported to death camps, and 15,000 had escaped to join the Polish resistance.

In August 1944, the Soviet Red Army advanced to within 8 miles (13 km) of Warsaw. The Polish Home Army, a partisan group supported by the Polish government in exile in London, rose in revolt and captured three-fifths of the city. However, the Red Army had overstretched itself and was soon pushed back 60 miles (100 km) by the Germans. With the Red Army unable

RECOLLECTION

"The hour of action has struck ... By fighting in the streets of Warsaw, we shall bring nearer the moment of ultimate liberation ..."

Radio broadcast in Polish from Moscow, July 29, 1944.

to break through, the Germans crushed the uprising at the cost of more than 200,000 Polish lives. Only 15,000 Polish fighters survived the uprising; the Germans granted them prisoner of war status and marched them all off to prison camps.

The Warsaw Uprising is one of the most controversial events of the war. Some have argued that the Soviet leader, Stalin, encouraged a premature uprising in the knowledge it would fail, because he supported the rival communist Polish People's Army and not the Polish Home Army. A similarly premature Slovakian uprising in August 1944 was also brutally crushed.

Liberation

As Allied troops moved across Europe toward Germany—the Soviets from the east, the U.S., British, Canadian, and other troops from the west and south—they liberated towns and cities that had been under occupation for up to seven years. The response they met almost everywhere was one of jubilation. People poured out of their houses to celebrate their freedom. Now that the war was over, they could live their lives as before.

Liberation could not come soon enough for these women and young children liberated by Soviet soldiers from Auschwitz. If the liberation had occured a few days later, many of them would have died or been sent on "death marches" to camps in Germany.

For some, liberation could not have come soon enough. In the east, Soviet troops entered Auschwitz on January 27, 1945; it was the first death camp to be liberated. They found 7,650 Jews still alive. Other camps were empty, since all remaining Jews had either been killed or sent on death marches westward toward camps in Germany. Those Jews and resistance fighters lucky enough to have avoided detection by the Germans emerged from the attics and cellars in which they had taken refuge, or came down from the mountains and forests in which they had lived like outlaws for the past four or more years.

For the Dutch, the Channel Islanders, and others, liberation brought relief from hunger. As the Allies swept across Europe, groups of retreating German troops became trapped or isolated. Food quickly ran out during the harsh winter of 1944–45, and the local populations soon starved. The eventual liberation of the Netherlands on April 28, 1945 allowed Allied planes to drop much-needed food and medical supplies to the starving population.

For others, liberation was far from welcome. Many people living in the east feared the advancing Red Army almost as much as they did the Nazis, for the Soviet troops had a barbaric reputation for rape and other brutalities. Red Army troops who had been taken prisoner by the Germans also feared for their lives, as the Soviet leader, Stalin, considered them potential counterrevolutionaries because of their possible contamination by Nazi or Western

Advancing Allied troops in western Europe were greeted everywhere by local people as liberators. They were especially welcomed by children when, as here in the Netherlands, they also handed out chocolate and sweets.

ideas. Of the 5.5 million Russians returned home from Germany in 1945–46, 1.5 million Red Army troops, including 11 of 37 captured generals, were sent to labor camps in Siberia by Stalin. Russian civilians taken by force to work in Germany were watched when they returned by the NKVD as "*potential enemies of the state*" and were forbidden to go within 60 miles (100 km) of cities such as Moscow.

One group of people in particular dreaded liberation. Across Europe, thousands of people had collaborated with the Nazis. Partisans or the resistance shot many of these, including Mussolini, and others were jailed or publicly humiliated. Women collaborators who had slept with German soldiers had their heads shaven to show their betrayal.

RECOLLECTION

"… fifteen solid miles of cheering, deliriously happy people waiting to shake your hand, to kiss you, to shower you with food and wine."

Liberation was as glorious for the troops as it was for the local citizens, as this description of the liberation of Paris reveals.

U.S. Major Frank Burk in Paris, August 25, 1944.

Aftermath

The end of occupation brought liberation and a host of problems. Towns and cities needed rebuilding, industry and agriculture restarted, and people resettled after war's turmoil.

Each freed country established a new government. In the Netherlands and Norway, heads of state returned from exile and restored democracy. France devised a new republican constitution in 1946. Italy restored the democracy that had been abolished by Mussolini, and voted to become a republic in 1946. In central Europe, the Czechs hoped to return to their prewar democratic constitution, and many Poles wanted their government in exile in London to return. Stalin had different ideas, installing pro-Soviet communist governments across all of central and Eastern Europe by 1948. Communist partisans seized power in Yugoslavia and Albania.

The victorious Allies (the U.S., the Soviet Union, Britain, and France) occupied Germany and Austria, each running its own area. In 1949, Britain, France, and the U.S. merged their German zones to create the democratic West Germany, and the Soviet-controlled east became a communist state. A democratic government was set up in Austria in 1945. In 1955, Austria proclaimed itself to be a neutral nation. The U.S. occupied Japan, and devised a democratic constitution for the country in 1946 with Emperor Hirohito remaining as head of state. In Southeast Asia, the European powers returned to run their colonies; however, all these colonies had gained their independence by 1963.

Across Europe, collaborators were shot or put on trial. In France, 170,000 collaborators, including Marshal Pétain, head of the Vichy state, stood trial. Denmark, Belgium, and the Netherlands were also vigorous in bringing collaborators to trial. Although the war had ended, rebuilding the peace was far from painless.

Leading Nazi officials stood trial for war crimes at Nuremberg from 1945 to 1949. Out of 21 leading Nazis, 11 were sentenced to death. Here, accused war criminals are guarded by U.S. military police.

TIMELINE

1939

August	Nazi-Soviet nonaggression pact agreed.
September	Germany invades Poland.
September	World War II begins as Britain and France declare war on Germany.

1940

April	Germany invades Denmark and Norway.
May	Germany invades Netherlands, Belgium, and Luxembourg.
May	Winston Churchill becomes British prime minister.
May	German troops cross French frontier.
June	General de Gaulle broadcasts to the French from London.
June	France surrenders to Germany.
June	German troops begin to occupy Channel Islands.
July	Churchill sets up Special Operations Executive to conduct sabotage in Europe.

1941

April	Germany invades Yugoslavia and Greece.
April	Soviet Union signs neutrality pact with Japan.
June	Operation Barbarossa: Germany invades Soviet Union.
July	Japanese occupy French Indo-China.
December	Japan attacks U.S. fleet at Pearl Harbor; U.S. enters the war.
December	Japan attacks Philippines, Malaya, and Thailand.
December	Germany declares war on U.S.

1942

January	Japan attacks Dutch East Indies and Burma.
January	Nazis plan the "Final Solution" at Wannsee Conference.
February	British surrender Singapore to the Japanese.
April–May	Battle of Coral Sea halts Japanese advance in southwest Pacific.
May	First Jews gassed at Auschwitz.
May	Czech resistance fighters assassinate Reinhard Heydrich in Prague.
June	U.S. fleet defeats Japanese at Battle of Midway.
October–November	British defeat German and Italian armies at El Alamein in north Africa.
November	Allies invade Vichy-held north Africa in Operation Torch.
November	German troops occupy Vichy France.

1943

February	Germans defeated at Stalingrad.
July	Allies invade Italy.
July	Mussolini overthrown.
September	Italy surrenders; Germans occupy country.
November	Italian anti-fascist partisans unite to fight German occupation.
November	Churchill, Roosevelt, and Stalin meet in Tehran, Persia, to plan Allied invasion of western Europe.
December	British aid Tito's partisans in Yugoslavia.

1944

June	D-Day: Allies land on Normandy beaches to begin liberation of France.
August–October	Warsaw uprising.
October	Communist partisans liberate Albania.
October	U.S. troops invade Japanese-held Philippines.
October	Tito's partisans and Red Army liberate Belgrade.

1945

March	U.S. troops finally take strategic Japanese island of Iwo Jima.
April	Italian partisans capture and kill Mussolini.
May	Germany surrenders.
May	Germans surrender on Channel Islands.
August	The U.S. drops atomic bomb on Hiroshima.
August	Japan surrenders.

GLOSSARY

Anti-Semitism
Prejudice against Jewish people.

Armistice
Agreement between opposing sides to cease fire while a peace agreement is reached.

Authoritarian
Describes a political system where obedience to a ruling person or group is enforced.

Cavalcade
A spectacular series or procession of things or people.

Collaborator
Someone who works with and for the enemy.

Combatant
Person, group, or country engaged in an armed struggle against an enemy.

Communism
The theory of an economic and social system in which everyone is equal and where all property is owned collectively, by the people.

Concentration camp
Prison camp where Jews and others were held in captivity and often worked to death.

Conscription
Compulsory military service or work in industry or civil defense.

Constitution
Written document setting out principles on which a country is founded and the rights its people enjoy.

Courier
A person that carries and delivers packages or diplomatic correspondence.

Curfew
A restriction on people's movements, requiring them to stay indoors after a certain time.

Death camp
Also called an extermination camp, where Jews and others were systematically killed, usually by poison gas.

Democracy
Government by the people or their elected representatives in parliament.

Deport
To expel or remove someone from a country.

Dictator
A leader who takes complete control of a country and often rules by force.

Einsatzgruppen
"Action groups" of SS troops who murdered enemies of the Nazis, notably Jews and communists.

Encipher
To convert a message into code.

Fascism
An extreme political movement based on nationalism and, usually, military authority that aims to unite a country's people into a disciplined force under an all-powerful leader.

"Final Solution"
The "final solution of the Jewish question," the German phrase used to describe the extermination of all Jews in Europe.

Ghetto
A poor part of town where Jews and others were forced to live.

Guerrilla
A member of an unofficial, usually politically motivated armed force.

Holocaust
Deliberate attempt by the Nazis to kill all Jews in Europe.

Interned
When a person is detained or confined against his or her will by an enemy or occupying force in a prison camp.

Labor camp
Work camp using slave labor, mostly Jews and prisoners of war, to produce materials for the German war effort.

Nationalist
Person who is passionately loyal to his or her own country.

Nazi Party
Extreme fascist party led by Adolf Hitler that ruled Germany from 1933–45; Nazi is an abbreviated term for the National Socialist German Workers' Party.

Neutral
Describes a nation that refuses to take sides in a war and does not fight.

Partisan
Member of an armed resistance group fighting inside a country against an invading or occupying army.

Puppet state
One state controlled by another

Red Army
Army of the Soviet Union.

Rotor
A rotating part of a machine.

Scuttle
To deliberately sink a ship or fleet to prevent it falling into enemy hands

Soviet Union
Union of the Soviet Socialist Republics (U.S.S.R.). A communist state that existed from 1922–91.

SS
Schutzstaffel, or "protection squads," originally Hitler's personal bodyguard but later expanded into a vast organization responsible for killing enemies of the state; it also had a military wing, the *Waffen SS.*

Third Reich
Name given to Nazi rule in Germany; *reich* is German for "empire."

T4 "euthanasia program"
A Nazi program, between 1939-41, during which the Nazis systematically killed people with mental and physical disabilities.

U-boat
German submarine used in WWI and WWII.

FURTHER INFORMATION

FURTHER READING

Documenting WWII: The Eastern Front by Simon Adams, Rosen Young Adult, 2008

Documenting WWII: The Holocaust by Neil Tonge, Rosen Young Adult, 2008

Documenting WWII: War in the Pacific by Sean Sheehan, Rosen Young Adult, 2008

World War II by Simon Adams, DK Children, 2007

World War II: Europe by Margaret J Goldstein, Lerner Publications, 2004

Web Sites
Due to the changing nature of Internet links, Rosen Publishing has developed an online list of Web Sites related to the subject of this book. This site is regularly updated. Please use this link to access this list:
http://www.rosenlinks.com/dww/ocre

PLACES TO VISIT

United States Holocaust Memorial Museum, 100 Raoul Wallenberg Place, SW Washington, D.C. 20024-2126

U.S. Air Force Museum, 1100 Spaatz Street, Wright-Patterson Air Force Base, Ohio 45433

U.S.S. Arizona, 1 Arizona Memorial Place, Honolulu, Hawaii 96818
Memorial and museum commemorating the Japanese attack on Pearl Harbor.

INDEX

Numbers in **bold** refer to illustrations.